the extreme sports collection

bicycle stunt riding!

catch air

by Chris Hayhurst

rosen publishing group's
rosen central
new york

Published in 2000 by The Rosen Publishing Group, Inc.
29 East 21st Street, New York, NY 10010

Copyright © 2000 by The Rosen Publishing Group, Inc.

First Edition

Library of Congress Cataloging-in-Publication Data

Hayhurst, Chris.
    Bicycle stunt riding / Chris Hayhurst.
       p.   cm. — (Extreme sports collection)
    Includes bibliographical references (p. 61) and index.
    Summary: Describes the sport of bicycle stunt riding, how to purchase equipment, practice stunts, ride safely, and enter competitions.
    ISBN 0-8239-3011-4 (lib. bdg.)
    1. Bicycle motocross Juvenile literature. 2. Stunt cycling Juvenile literature.
[1. Bicycle motocross. 2. Stunt cycling.] I. Title. II. .Series.
GV1049.3.H29   1999
796.6—dc21   99-36847
                                                      CIP

2

contents

Let's get something straight: What's extreme to you might not be extreme to the next person. And what's extreme to that person might be tame to you. You see, the word "extreme" is relative. It means something different for everybody.

One thing everyone can agree on, however, is that when it comes to extreme sports, bicycle stunt riding definitely qualifies. Also known as freestyle biking, the sport involves using a BMX (bicycle motocross) bicycle to get big air and perform radical tricks. It requires lots of talent and creativity. What the freestyle cyclist tries is limited only by his or her imagination.

Like many sports, bicycle stunt riding has changed over time. Twenty years ago, all you had to do to be extreme in the world of biking was to be a BMX racer. Pulling off big tricks and jumps wasn't even a part of the sport. Some riders would try tricks during a race, but their goal was always to win the race, not to do the hardest stunts. Back then, if you mentioned

stunt jumping, it was likely that no one would know what you were talking about. If you were jumping or doing tricks, you were living on the edge. You were extreme just because you were different.

Today it's not that simple. Many people ride freestyle. To be an extreme rider nowadays, you not only need to have a freestyle bicycle, but you also have to know how to do wild tricks while you ride it. You have to ride hard, fast, and high. You have to pull off spins and twists and use obstacles to demonstrate your control and finesse on the bike. Finally, you have to be able to pick yourself up after a crash, dust yourself off, and try it all over again. That's extreme.

BMX racers are extreme athletes who pedal their way through mud and over dirt jumps.

Today there are the X Games, a sort of miniature Olympics for extreme sports. Athletes from around the world gather for this event to show just how extreme they can be. They climb walls of ice; race down slippery, snow-covered ski slopes on mountain bikes; and jump out of airplanes with skateboards strapped to their feet. They compete to see who can grab the biggest air, who can hit the highest speeds, and who can perform the most

Extreme Fact
According to *USA Today*, bicycling is an incredibly popular sport. An estimated 47.9 million people ride bikes every year!

difficult stunts. The winners are given gold medals and the title of "Most Extreme Athlete on the Planet." Most extreme, that is, until the next X Games, when new athletes will redefine what it means to be extreme. Another version of extreme sports takes place behind-the-scenes, away from the glory that comes with television coverage and cheering crowds. These athletes prefer to play in the woods or on a quiet street, alone with nature or with a couple of friends. They're the mountain climbers, the backcountry snowboarders and skiers, the explorers. Among stunt riders, they're the majority—the ones who use homemade halfpipes and ramps in their backyards to do tricks that only they and their friends will ever witness. They'll never get a gold medal for what they do, and they probably wouldn't want one anyway. They're doing what they do because they love it, not because it attracts a crowd.

Most people agree that for a sport to be extreme, it has to be difficult—at least for the beginner. It must require specialized skills and techniques. It also requires an adventurous attitude—the kind of attitude that says there are no limits. Whether this means launching into a 360-degree spin as you fly over a dirt jump, letting go of the handlebars as you soar into the sky, or just lifting your front wheel off the ground for the first time, it all depends on who you are and what you're willing, or not willing, to try.

Biker Bio

What does it take to win three gold medals at a single X Games? Ask Dave Mirra. Known to his friends as "Miracle Boy," Mirra did just that by winning the 1998 X Games Singles Vert, Doubles Vert, and Street competitions. But that's not all. In the 1999 X Games, Mirra came back again to win golds in Vert and Street. In the process, he pulled off a few extremely radical tricks: A 540 X-out, a truck driver, flairs, and even a no-handed to no-footed back flip. What does that look like? You'll have to watch Mirra the next time he competes, as he's one of the only people in the world who can do it.

Known for his technical precision as well as the occasional big trick, it's no wonder that "Miracle Boy" Mirra is considered by many fellow riders to be the best bicycle stunt rider on the planet.

Extreme sports can be dangerous, but being extreme doesn't mean being foolish or taking unnecessary risks. No bicycle stunt rider wants to risk an injury that might mean never riding again. You can be extreme and still follow safety rules.

If you think that you want to be extreme but you're not sure where to start, try freestyle biking. You'll find an adventure with every jump and trick. In freestyle cycling, you can be as extreme as you want to be.

Extreme Beginnings

The first Extreme Games, later known as the X Games, were held in 1995 in Rhode Island. It attracted more than 350 world-class athletes. That year the events included bungee jumping, barefoot water-ski jumping, windsurfing, skysurfing, street luge, skateboarding, mountain biking, and—you guessed it—bicycle stunt riding. In 1998, only three years later, almost a quarter of a million people attended the Summer X Games.

Considering how popular bicycle stunt riding is today, it's hard to imagine a world without it. Just a few short decades ago, no one had even heard of the sport. In fact, back then your friends would have thought that you were crazy if you suggested performing back flips and helicopter spins atop a bicycle. Bounce up and down on your front wheel? Forget about it!

There is very little history

written about the rise of freestyle biking, but one thing is certain. The sport owes its very existence to the dirt bike. Motorcycle motocross, as the sport of dirt biking is known, involves racing a modified motorcycle around a jump-filled dirt track at high speeds. The best riders are able to rip around the course without ever falling off, and they often catch fantastic air each time they hit a jump.

It sounds like fun, but motorcycle motocross is for adults only. In the early 1970s, however, a crew of speed-hungry kids in southern California decided to invent a bike-racing sport of their own: BMX, or bicycle motocross. These kids took their Schwinn Stingray bicycles (the most popu-

lar bike back then), made a few minor changes to them so that they'd be sturdy enough for off-road riding, and pedaled for the dirt. Soon tracks were made, and jumps were built. The only differences between BMX and motorcycle motocross were the bikes, the engines, and the speed. BMX riders, decked out in motorcycle helmets, body padding, and gloves, could compete against one another in organized races around the country. Or they could just take to the neighborhood track whenever they felt like it. The sport literally took off.

From Racing to Stunt Riding

What does all of this have to do with bicycle stunt riding? Well, in a word: air. Big air. By the 1980s, many BMX racers were trying to go as high as they could each time they hit a jump. Some of them were even trying tricks. At the same time, some BMXers began taking their bikes to skateboard parks where they could experiment on ramps and in halfpipes. Soon an entirely new sport evolved—freestyle riding.

By the mid-1980s, freestyle riding had hit the big time. Competitions were held in skateboard parks, and riders would show off their best tricks. They would compete to see who could fly the highest and pull the most radical stunts. Since then, more and bigger competitions have been created—such as the X Games bicycle stunt event. Riders are constantly pushing the envelope when it comes to both aerial stunts and street performances. Competitors hailing from around the world can now do tricks on their freestyle bikes that were once considered to be impossible. With each new trick, stunt riders raise the bar in terms of technical difficulty and all-out high-flying courage. And with every new rider, the sport becomes more popular. What's in store for the future of bicycle stunt riding is anybody's guess, but one thing is for sure: It will definitely be extreme.

Extreme Fact
Dave Mirra is the proud owner of ten X Games medals: eight golds and two silvers.

Biker Bio

Jay Miron, a stunt biker better known as the Canadian Beast, may be second only to Dave Mirra when it comes to all-out extreme stunt-biking ability. Miron finished right behind Mirra in both the Vert and Street competitions of the 1999 X Games. Hailing from Thunder Bay, Ontario, and now living in British Columbia, Miron landed a 540 tail whip to edge out third-place finisher Simon Tabron. He also managed a cloud-busting Superman seat grab that got the crowd roaring. With his knack for big air and his ability to pull difficult tricks like these, sooner or later Miron is bound to take home the gold.

When it comes to equipment, bicycle stunt riding is a simple sport. In fact, the only thing you really need to get rolling is a bike. Freestyle bikes are made differently from normal street bikes. They're usually a lot heavier, weighing in at a hefty thirty to forty pounds. They also come with a few features not ordinarily found on your typical rig: small wheels, upright handlebars, supergrip pedals, and metal foot pegs that can be used for performing tricks. Many bikes have special brakes designed for the needs of the freestyle rider.

Knowing What You Want

Before you spend a small fortune—from $200 to as much as

$1,000—on a brand-new freestyle bike, try to figure out exactly what you're looking for. What do you need? If you're a beginner, chances are you won't need the latest top-of-the-line model. You can probably get by with an inexpensive bike, something that can serve as a good introduction to the sport. You may even wish to buy a used bike. Used bikes are always cheaper than new ones and are often just as good.

If you have a friend who is already into bicycle stunt riding, ask this person if you can borrow his or her bike for a test spin. See if you like it. If it feels comfortable, it might be the bike for you. Test-ride as many bikes as you can before you actually buy anything. Most bike shops will let you pedal around the store parking lot until you're sure that you've found the right machine.

Once you're ready to buy, make sure that you consider your options. It's always wise to shop around. Visit all the bike stores in town to see what's on sale. Scope out the classified section of your

Stunt riders show their stuff at the 1998 X Games.

local paper. Surf the Internet for good deals on second-hand bikes. Soon you'll have the rig of your dreams.

Bike Basics

Most freestyle bike frames are made of high-tensile cro-moly, a strong type of steel that can withstand all the pounding that comes with stunt riding. The wheels—twenty inches in diameter instead of the twenty-six inches found on a mountain bike—are generally made of a lighter but equally strong aluminum alloy. The seat, or "saddle," of a freestyle bike can either be well padded—a welcome feature for those who tend to have hard landings—or not.

To get the whole rig spinning, there are aluminum pedals. The pedals come with clawlike spikes designed to grip the soles of your shoes. Any shoe with a stiff bottom will do when you're just starting out. When your feet aren't on the pedals or in the air, they're on the pegs. The pegs stick out from the wheel axle about three or four inches on either side. There are two sets of pegs—one for the front wheel and one for the rear wheel—on every bike.

Extreme Fact
Freestyle bicycle seats are usually made out of extremely hard plastic—not exactly the most comfortable material for sitting on. But that's just fine for most freestyle riders, who tend to spend more time standing on their pedals, balancing on their pegs, and just plain flying than sitting on the seat.

brake handle

pedal

pegs

19

Bike-Sizing Tips

What size bike you should buy depends on your height and the length of your legs. You want to be sure to get a bike that is just right for your body. Otherwise it might be difficult to maneuver. Use the following chart to get an idea of what size frame you should look for. Remember, everybody is different. Ask the salesperson to help you pick exactly the right bike for your build and needs.

Height (feet-inches)	Frame Size
Under 5'4"	12.5–14.5
5'4" to 5'8"	16
5'8" to 5'11"	18
5'11" to 6'	19–20
Over 6'	20–22

The last—and some might say the most important—feature on a freestyle bike is the braking system. The simplest bikes come with standard "caliper" brakes, the same type of brakes as any other bike. But on freestyle bikes, they have extralong cables to allow handlebar-spinning tricks. Fancier models come with a "gyro," a gadget that allows the brakes to spin freely no matter what trick is being performed. Gyros are helpful because you never have to worry about tangling up your brake cables as you pull off extreme moves.

Smart Shopping Tips

Looking for a great deal on a used bike? Try scanning the classified section of your local newspaper. You'll often find secondhand gear at affordable prices. If you don't find what you need there, go on-line. There are many Internet sites that are bound to have what you need. To get started, try logging on to *http://www.bicycletrader.com*. Finally, if the Internet doesn't get you wired, go to a bike store. In addition to their regular inventory of new bikes, many stores carry used rigs as well.

Bicycle stunt riding is a hot sport. More and more people are trying it every day. There's one thing you can be sure of: You won't be alone if you're just starting out. That's one of the best things about freestyle riding—it's a great way to spend time with your friends.

Getting started in the world of freestyle riding is easy. Just build a huge jump at the bottom of the biggest hill you can find, and then down you go. But wait just one minute! You forgot something. First you have to find the right bike.

A stunt biker drops into the half-pipe in Woodward Camp, Pennsylvania.

The Right Bike

Give your local bike store a call. If you're not sure if there's a bike shop in your town, check the phone book. You'll probably find at least one or two listed in the Yellow Pages under "Bicycles." When you find a shop that sells freestyle bikes, stroll on over for a visit. Bike store salespeople can be very helpful when it comes to deciding which bike is right for you. They can also help you pick out a good helmet as well as other safety gear, such as shin and knee guards. If they don't have what you need, they can probably tell you where to get it. They may even have ideas on where you can find a used bike or where you can meet other beginning freestyle riders.

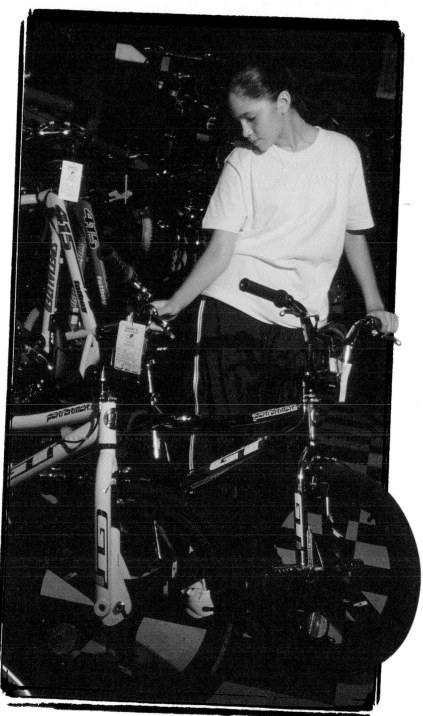

Whatever you do, be sure to ask a lot of questions. Are you sure that you can afford this thing? Can you find a better bike, used, for less money? Have you shopped around for special deals and asked your friends for their opinions? Have you test-ridden their bikes to see if you like them? When you've done all this and are sure that you know what you want, purchase your bike. Now it's time to get radical.

Getting Started

You can begin anywhere you like. That's one of the best things about bicycle stunt riding. Freestyle means freedom. All you need is a little space—maybe the size of a small parking lot or your driveway—to experiment. Ride slowly. Try shifting your weight around to get a feel for how the bike handles and how it responds to your body. Play with the brakes. Try sitting on the bike without moving at all. Stay at a complete standstill without taking your feet off the pedals. Stand on the pegs. Balance on one peg. Now you're getting to know your bike. You're getting a feel for how you and your bike can work together.

Believe it or not, becoming familiar with your bike is the most important

step you can take when you're just getting started. Once riding your stunt bike comes as easily as walking, you can head for the dirt jumps, the half-pipes, and the riding parks. There you'll discover the true meaning of "extreme."

Don't fence me in! This stunt rider attacks a chain-link fence in Woodland Hills, California.

Tune Time

Many bike shops offer customers a free tune-up when they buy a new bike. Just buy the bike, ride it for a few months, and then bring it back to the shop. The mechanic will tweak, oil, and align all the components and put everything back into tip-top shape. When you're shopping for a bike, ask the salesperson what the store's policy is on tune-ups and maintenance.

5 Safe Biking

Bicycle stunt riding can be very dangerous. The fact is, many of the best tricks involve launching—bike, body, and all—high into the air. Should you misjudge or mess up the landing, as often happens, you'll crash. When you crash, you run the risk of injury. Sometimes those injuries can be quite serious.

Kris Bennet gets airborne over a dirt jump at the 1997 X Games.

Protecting Yourself

Fortunately you can take a few precautions to ensure that when you do crash, you don't get hurt. The most important thing you can do is to wear a helmet. Some bikers wear simple skateboard-style helmets. Others prefer regular bike helmets. Still others go for motorcycle-style helmets that protect the entire face as well as the head. If you're planning on making big jumps, head and face protection is necessary. Make sure that your helmet fits well. It should be snug and should include straps to keep it on your head in case you fly upside down.

In addition to a helmet, many stunt bikers wear shin guards, elbow

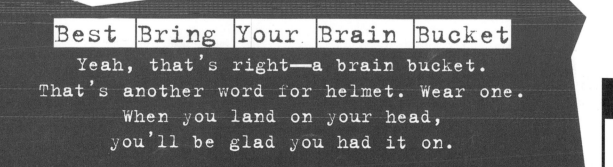

Best Bring Your Brain Bucket
Yeah, that's right—a brain bucket.
That's another word for helmet. Wear one.
When you land on your head,
you'll be glad you had it on.

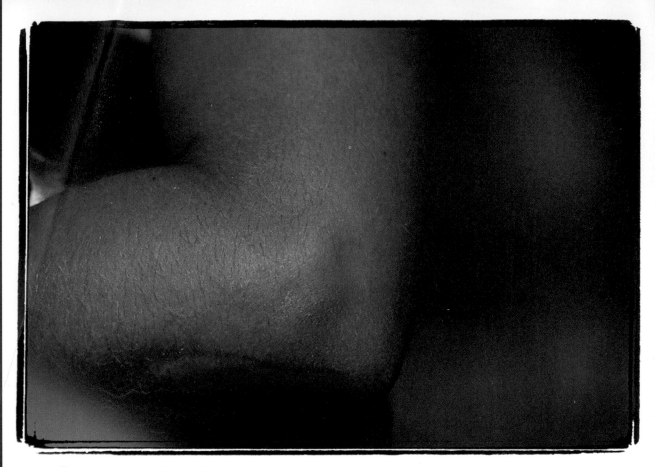

Ouch! This biker sports a 'swelbo' from riding without elbow pads.

pads, and knee pads. These guards and pads come in handy when you skid across blacktop or when the bike lands on top of you as you attempt a trick. Bikers wear padded gloves to protect against painful palm rubs across the pavement. The truth is, by the time a stunt biker is fully outfitted, he or she looks more like an armored knight ready for battle than an athlete prepared for the extreme.

Extreme Fact
The average freestyle bike weighs between thirty and forty pounds. By comparison, some racing bikes—the sleek machines you see in the Tour de France—weigh less than twenty pounds.

Mark "Gonz" Gonzales does a fakie wall ride.

If you don't feel that all that padding protecting your head and body is enough, don't fear. Most freestyle bikes come with some padding right on the bike itself. Standard pads can be found on the top tube of the frame and around the stem, the two spots you are most likely to smack into in an accident. Many seats, too, come with a little extra cushion just where you need it.

Brake Business

One thing is for sure: To ride safely, you've got to have good brakes. If your brakes aren't working as well as you'd like them to, try the following:

- Clean the wheel rims. A little rubbing alcohol and some gentle brushwork with steel wool will do the trick.
- Sand the brake pads with a piece of sandpaper. This should add a little texture to the pads, and texture means better gripping power.
- Make sure that your brake pads are centered and aligned with your wheel rims.
- Bring your bike into the shop. A bike mechanic should be able to help you out.

Safety in the Streets

Even if aerials aren't your cup of tea, that doesn't necessarily mean that you should have no safety concerns. Street riding can be dangerous, especially when cars are around. Make sure that you know the rules of the road if you're going to take your bike out on the street, and always obey all traffic laws. If you're going to ride in a freestyle park, beware of other riders, bystanders, and additional obstacles.

Above all, use common sense. Never try a trick that is obviously beyond your ability. Even the best riders practice for years before they can pull off the most difficult stunts. If you're patient and ride within your limits, you're bound to improve. Try the "easy" stuff first. Then when you're ready, move on to more challenging maneuvers. Before you know it, you'll be performing radical tricks and, if you're careful, doing so in one piece.

Rules of the Road

Every town on city has its own rules and regulations when it comes to where you can and cannot ride. In some towns, for example, you might not be permitted to use sidewalk curbs for doing tricks. Other towns have specially designated freestyle parks—used by skaters and bikers—where you can pull off as many stunts as you like. Still others don't allow riding at night without a light or riding at any time without a helmet. Whatever the rules, they're usually established for safety reasons. Make sure that you obey your local laws.

One of the trickiest things about bicycle stunt riding—aside from the tricks themselves—is deciding where and how to ride. You can pretty much try moves anywhere you like, as long as you're careful not to bother anybody.

Cruising down the sidewalk? Throw on the brakes and rock onto your front wheel for an endo. Cranking over the dirt-bike trails? Grab huge air off the rollers. Once you've got your wheels spinning, there's almost no limit to the things you can do and the places you can go.

This stunt biker makes a bar spin look easy at the Burning Bike Festival in Phoenix, Arizona.

The Endo and the Hop

Here are two simple beginner's stunts to get you started: the endo and the hop. The endo is sort of like a backward wheelie. Start by rolling your bike slowly toward a curb. When your front tire hits the curb, push forward on your handlebars and throw your weight up and to the front of your bike. Your rear wheel should come up off the ground so that you're balancing only on your front wheel. After holding that position for a second or two, rock back and drop your rear wheel down to the ground. If there's no curb around, you can still try this move. Just roll forward until you're ready to go and then lock your front brake. Your front wheel will stop short just as if it had hit a curb.

The bunny hop is a simple trick used all the time by even the best freestyle riders. The idea is to lift both wheels off the ground at the same time, without the aid of a ramp or jump. All you need to do to make it work is to pull straight up on the handlebars while taking your weight off the seat and pedals. Go ahead and try it. In no time at all, you'll be bouncing like a rabbit.

The Lawn Mower

This is an excellent stunt to teach balance, and the technique is used in many other tricks. Roll forward very slowly while standing on the back pegs. Hit both brakes hard and do a small endo. When the rear wheel hits the ground, put your right foot on top of the rear wheel and push the bike to the right while pulling your body to the left. Take your left hand off the handlebars and with your right hand, twist the handlebars 180 degrees clockwise. You must lean away from the bike, or you will fall toward it and won't be able to maintain control. If you do this right, your weight will pull the bike up toward you, and you will be able to ride out of the stunt.

Trick Talk

Looking for a way to impress your friends? Try a kickout. It's a relatively simple trick performed while you're in the air. After takeoff, stand up a bit so that your butt comes off the seat, then use your legs and hips to swing the back of your bike out to the side. When you notice your buddy's mouth drop open, calmly reel the bike back in, get everything aligned, and make a nice, gentle landing.

The Whiplash

The whiplash is a fun stunt that can be done in either direction. While rolling, switch your body to the left side of the bike with your left foot on the front left peg and your right foot on the left rear peg. Push the frame of the bike around to the right with your right foot. At the same time, lean your chest forward and pull your left foot backward. As the bike spins halfway around, switch feet, from your left foot on the front left peg to your right foot on the front right peg. When the frame comes all the way around, put your left foot on top of the frame and ride out of the stunt.

Forward Rope-a-Roni

Learn to do the whiplash before attempting this trick. Roll forward with your body on the left side of the bike, with your right foot on the front left peg and your left foot on the left rear peg. Kick the frame around as with a whiplash. At the halfway point, let the back tire hit the ground and put your left foot on the right rear peg. Tap the rear brakes and pull the bike up onto the back tire, taking your right foot off the front peg. Release the brakes and let the bike coast in a tightening spiral. Just before your forward momentum is lost, hit the back brakes, untwist the handlebars, and ride away.

Freak Squeak

Many people now call a freak squeak a front yard, but with a front yard, both legs are in front of the handlebars, whereas with a freak squeak, your legs are straddling the bars. Begin by rolling forward with your left foot down and right foot up on the pedals. Bring your right leg over the handlebars and touch it to the front wheel. Without hitting your brakes, move your left foot to the front left peg. Press down with your right foot to raise the back wheel. Take both hands off the handlebars and scuff ahead with your right foot. Scuffing means to push one of the tires with your foot while the other wheel is off the ground. Then put both hands on the handlebars again, push the front wheel with your right foot, bring your right foot back over the handlebars, and ride away.

Elephant Glide

The elephant glide is a front wheel trick. Roll forward in a normal manner. Press your right pedal down and lift your left foot over the handlebars and onto the front left peg. Start circling to the left. Extending your right hand for balance, bring your right leg over the right grip and put it on top of the front tire. The back wheel should lift off the ground and come around to your right side. Grab the back of the seat with your right hand and begin scuffing the tire, with your left hand on the handlebars. Grab the back brakes or press down hard on the front wheel to get the back end of the bike to fall. Put your right foot on the back right peg while you sit on the handlebars. Then hit the back brakes hard, lean forward, and take your left foot off the front peg. You will be lifted onto the back wheel of the bike. Take your left hand off the grip and twist to the right. Straighten the handlebars and ride out of the stunt.

Day Smith is one of the best flatland stunt riders today.

Mega Spin

This is an advanced trick that will take time to learn. Roll forward with both feet on the back pegs. Take your right foot off the peg and turn your body slightly to the right. As your right foot moves behind you, the bike should be spinning to the right. Put your right foot on the rear tire and pull down hard, twisting the handle-bars slightly to the left. Correct technique and balance determine how much of a spin you can get out of this stunt. You have to learn how your bike pivots and how to balance it properly.

Watching the Pros

One of the best places to see all of the various bicycle stunt-riding styles is at an organized competition. The X Games, for instance, has several different freestyle events. Dirt jumping involves rocketing down a steep ramp and then launching into the air from the lip of a six-foot-high jump. Once airborne, the rider has several seconds to try any trick he or she can think of, from back flips to handlebar spins. In the difficult flatland event, the rider keeps the bike almost stationary while demonstrating numerous tricks that require a keen sense of balance and coordination. In street riding, bikers pedal through a course full of obstacles such as ramps, rails, boxes, and quarter-pipes, using them to perform hard tricks, catch

monster air, and show off their technical abilities. And in the halfpipe event, also known as the vert, stunt bikers speed up and down the clifflike ramp walls, launching high into the sky with each run, or stalling at the lip to try challenging tricks. Some riders even pair up and enter the halfpipe together, and like synchronized swimmers, they demonstrate their acrobatic biking skills as a team.

No matter what the event, every freestyle routine is performed for a purpose: the chance to demonstrate thrilling moves. Whether airborne or firmly on the ground, what the bicycle stunt rider can do—or at least try to do—is limited only by his or her imagination. Creativity is everything.

Trick Talk

In the doubles vert competition, two riders assault the halfpipe ramp at the same time. Working together to create a trick-filled routine, the fearless pedallers ride in opposite directions while attempting to synchronize their aerials. Sometimes both riders will hop onto the same bike—one up front on the pedals, the other in back on the pegs. As you can imagine, one of the most difficult things about riding doubles is to avoid crashing into a moving obstacle. And when that moving obstacle is your teammate, you want to make doubly sure you don't hit it!

Freestyle biking is not easy. In fact, it may be one of the most difficult sports around. It requires balance, coordination, creativity, strength, and above all, discipline. Tricks can take days, months, and even years to learn. Whereas some moves can be picked up in no time with little stunt-riding experience, many others require extreme concentration and countless hours of practice. To get good, you have to ride a lot.

None of this should keep you from trying. When you start out, the most important thing is to make sure that you have fun. If this means just pedaling around the neighborhood, getting used to your bike and how it handles, that's fine. In time and with practice, you'll be doing tricks that once seemed impossible.

Start slowly. You can begin by mastering the so-called simple stuff. These are the things you see riders doing every time they get on their bikes, like endos, bunny hops, and bar spins. Learn how to stand on the foot pegs and how to move from one peg to the other. Try jumping curbs and speed bumps or other low obstacles. One of the best ways to learn these moves is by reading freestyle biking magazines and by renting videos on freestyle biking. Many video stores carry how-to movies featuring the top bicycle stunt-riding stars.

Eventually you'll start to get a good feel for your bike. Riding will begin to feel as natural as walking. When that happens, you'll know that you're ready to experiment with the big moves. Try building your own jumps out of wood, dirt, or whatever else you can find.

Learning More

For good articles explaining how to perform many different types of bicycle stunt-riding tricks, check out magazines like *Ride BMX*, *SNAP BMX*, and *Bike*. These magazines often include detailed instructions on how to do everything from the simplest maneuvers to the burliest tricks. They always have amazing photographs that are sure to get you pumped for your next session on the bike.

Remember, even the best pros have trouble doing many of the more difficult tricks. They often crash—and crash hard. As a beginner, you should never try to do anything that is beyond your ability. Not only can it be dangerous, but it can also be frustrating. So take it easy, and don't expect to do anything too extreme until you've put in the time.

Trick Talk

Have you ever tried a wheelie without pedaling? If you have, you've got another trick to add to your been-there-done-that list. It's called a manual. To do one, just pull back on your handlebars and throw your weight way back so that the front wheel comes off the ground. Then keeping your feet on the pedals, flex your knees in and out. If you have good balance, you should be able to keep rolling.

Biker Slang

What does it mean to be "limbless"? What does it mean to pull a "truck driver"? If you're new to the world of bicycle stunt riding, you may have trouble keeping up with all the terms used to describe various styles and tricks. Here are definitions of some of the words you're likely to hear around freestyle bikers.

Bar Spin Spinning the handlebars (and the front wheel) around in the air.

Bus Driver A one-handed bar spin.

Can Can Taking a foot off one pedal and crossing it over the top of the bike.

Candy Bar Taking a foot off one pedal and thrusting it over the handlebars.

Contort Twisting and turning one's body while keeping all limbs on the bike.

Cross-Up (X-Up) Turning the handlebars in one direction as far as possible without letting go.

Fakey Jumping facing one way and then landing facing the opposite direction.

Flip Just like it sounds—a somersault in the air with the bike.

Limbless Taking hands or feet off the bike, then returning them to their positions before landing.

No footer   Taking both feet off the pedals then thrusting them out to the sides of the bike as far as they can go.

No hander   Taking both hands off the handlebars and flinging them out to the sides of the bike as far as you can reach.

Nothing   Completely letting go of the bike with both hands and feet, then grabbing the bike again before landing.

Spin   Rotating with the bike like a helicopter propeller. A 360-degree spin involves one complete rotation. Other variations include 180s, 540s, and 720s.

Superman   Taking both feet off the pedals and stretching them as far behind the bike as possible while never letting go of the handlebars.

Tail whip   Holding on to the handlebars while lifting your butt off the seat and your feet off the pedals, and spinning the entire bike beneath you. Then you sit down again before you hit the ground.

Toboggan   Standing on the pedals while turning the handlebars sideways with one hand and holding the seat with the other.

Truck Driver   Performing a bus driver while completing a 360-degree spin.

If you've been riding freestyle even for a short while, chances are you've thought about competing against other bikers. Perhaps you've imagined what it would be like to win the gold at a major competition, or how it would feel to pull off your best trick in front of a group of screaming spectators.

Then again, maybe you haven't. Maybe competition isn't your thing. Perhaps you'd rather cruise around on your bike without the pressure of having to perform in front of a crowd. You might prefer to try tricks on your own or with a few friends. You would never—not in your entire life—enter a competitive event.

Either way, competition has something for everyone, whether as a competitor or as a spectator. If you go to compete, that's one thing. If you go for the food, music, and fun that come with a competition, that's OK too. Spending the entire day eating, listening to the tunes, and watching the pros throw big tricks can be just as much fun as competing.

Staging Your Own Event

If you're not sure if organized competition is for you, a good way to find out is by getting a few of your friends together for an informal showdown. You can build a ramp in your own backyard and stage a jumping competition. You can try a street-style comp in your driveway or in an empty parking lot. Even better, pedal over to the nearest skate park and test the waters there. Take turns doing tricks, and have spectators—or other friends—determine the winners.

If you're lucky, a small-scale freestyle event may already be scheduled in your area. If not, you can try to organize one yourself. All you really need to do is to put up signs in a couple of bike stores, invite a few local sponsors to supply food and music, and go out and have fun. If you pass the word around, people will come.

Professional Competition

If you decide that you want to compete on a larger scale, things become a
little more difficult. There is no national freestyle biking association, so
things are not as organized as in some other sports. Most major events
are for professionals: sponsored riders who make a living on their bikes.

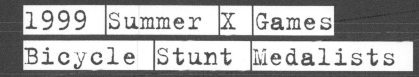

1999 Summer X Games Bicycle Stunt Medalists

Street
Gold: Dave Mirra
Silver: Jay Miron
Bronze: Chad Kagy

Vert
Gold: Dave Mirra
Silver: Jay Miron
Bronze: Simon Tabron

Flatland
Gold: Trevor Meyor
Silver: Phil Dolan
Bronze: Nathan Penonzek

Dirt Jump
Gold: T. J. Lavin
Silver: Brian Foster
Bronze: Ryan Nyquist

Extreme Fun

The annual MTV Sports and Music Festival is a three-day bonanza combining hot performances by well-known musicians like Rob Zombie and DMX with cutting-edge extreme sports. In addition to some of the world's best freestyle BMXers, the event attracts extreme skateboarders, in-line skaters, and others. If you're in the mood for sky-high air and an unforgettable concert or two, catch the show live in October. You can also wait a month for its appearance on MTV.

If you can't wait until the MTV show, check in at the summer Gravity Games, a four-day event staged in September. Held in Providence, Rhode Island, and sponsored by NBC, this sports and music festival features, among other entertainments, gravity-defying freestyle cyclists.

If that's not enough, try your luck at the X Trials or B3-Bikes, Boards, and Blades. These two events serve as warmups for the ESPN X Games and feature the best extreme athletes on the planet.

These events—such as the ESPN X Games, the MTV Sports and Music Festival, and the Gravity Games—all attract the world's best riders and draw thousands of spectators.

Unfortunately, at least for now, amateurs don't have as many options as the pros. Still, you can find the occasional amateur event, usually staged before or after a professional competition on the same jumps the pros use. Your best bet is to scan the freestyle BMX magazines for advertisements.

This biker grinds a handrail on his pegs.

When you find an event listed, give the organizer a call and ask about how you can enter.

If you do decide to compete, keep in mind the reason you started bicycle stunt riding in the first place: to have fun. When it comes down to it, the best thing about riding freestyle is the freedom of riding without limits. If you never forget that fact, you'll be sure to walk away from every competition with a smile on your face—and if you're lucky, a medal or two for your efforts.

Todd Lyons looks psyched and safe with his helmet on.

X-Planations

ABA   American Bicycle Association.

aerials   Tricks performed in the air.

BMX   Bicycle motocross.

brain bucket   Helmet.

burly   Big, as in "Did you see that burly trick?"

canyon   The dead space between jumping ramps.

catch air   To jump.

curb   To crash.

dirt   In the dirt-jumping competition, riders speed down an approach runway, launch off a dirt ramp for big air, then land on another, downward-sloping ramp.

face plant   To crash facefirst into the ground.

flatland   A competition that takes place without ramps or obstacles and that requires riders to demonstrate their technical skills and fancy footwork on a flat surface.

freestyle   A sport in which skill is based on an athlete's ability to come up with new and more extreme challenges.

halfpipe   A barrel-shaped ramp with high, curved sides and a flat bottom—perfect for high-flying aerials.

lip tricks   Tricks performed on the top edge of a ramp, like on the lip of a halfpipe.

lube Oil or grease used to lubricate bike components.

motocross Motorcycle racing done on a closed dirt and mud track.

pegs Short metal tubes that fasten to the front and rear axles of a freestyle bike and stick out on either side.

rig A bike.

vert The freestyle halfpipe competition, consisting of high-flying aerials and technical lip tricks.

Extreme Info

Web Sites

There are hundreds of freestyle BMX Web sites and other extreme sports pages on the Internet. Here are a few awesome sites to get you started:

The Bicycle Trader
http://www.bicycletrader.com

Bike Barn
http://www.bikebarn.com

The Bike Store
http://www.bicycles.org

BMXtra Online Magazine
http://www.bmxtra.com

Cyber Cyclery
http:www.cybercyclery.com

ESPN
http://www.espn.go.com/extreme/xgames

Extreme Sports Online
http://www.extreme-sports.com

GT Bicycles
http://www.gtbicycles.com

Hoffman Bicycles
http://www.hoffmanbikes.com

Internet Bicycling Hub
http://www.cyclery.com

Vans Shoes
http://www.vans.com

Organizations

There is no official body for the sport of freestyle BMX riding. The following three organizations are good sources of general bicycling information:

American Bicycle Association
P.O. Box 718
Chandler, AZ 85244
(602) 961-1903
Web site: http://www.ababmx.com

Bicycle Federation of America (BFA)
1818 R Street NW
Washington, DC 20009
(202) 332-6986
e-mail: bfa@igc.org

The National Bicycle League

3958 Brown Park Drive, Suite D

Hilliard, OH 43026

(614) 777-1625

e-mail: nbl@iwaynet.net

Web site: http://www.nbl.org

Camps

Most freestyle riders learn their tricks on their own or from friends. Usually they begin by competing in BMX races. (Contact the American Bicycle Association.) If you'd like to enroll in a camp and receive intensive guidance and training, contact:

Woodward Freestyle BMX Camp

P.O. Box 93

Route 45

Woodward, PA 16882

(814) 349-5633

e-mail: office@woodwardcamp.com

Web site: http://www.woodwardcamp.com

Extreme Reading

Books

Glaser, Jason. *Bicycle Stunt Riding.* Mankato, MN: Capstone Press, 1999.

Magazines

Bike
P.O. Box 1028
Dana Point, CA 92629
(949) 496-5922
e-mail: Bikemag@petersenpub.com

Ride BMX
1530 Brookhollow Drive, Suite A
Santa Ana, CA 92705
(714) 979-7688
Web site: http://www.ridebmxmag.com

SNAP BMX
1530 Brookhollow Drive, Suite A
Santa Ana, CA 92705
(714) 979-7688
e-mail: snapmag@aol.com
Web site: http://www.snapbmxmag.com

Index

Credits

About the Author

Chris Hayhurst is a freelance writer and photographer who specializes in the outdoors, sports, and environmental issues. In his spare time, he enjoys hiking, rock climbing, telemark skiing, and anything that takes him into the backcountry. He lives in Santa Fe, New Mexico.

Photo Credits

Series Design and Layout

Oliver H. Rosenberg

Consulting Editor

Jake Goldberg